# Fire Your Fear™

**How to Grow Your Business by Changing the Way You Think**

Deirdre Van Nest

Copyright © 2010 Deirdre Van Nest FIRE YOUR FEAR, LLC. All rights reserved. No portion of this book may be reproduced mechanically, electronically, or by any other means, including photocopying, without written permission of the publisher. It is illegal to copy this book, post it to a website, or distribute it by any other means without permission from the publisher.

Fire Your Fear, LLC
Edina, MN
coach@fireyourfear.com
www.fireyourfear.com

Limits of Liability and Disclaimer of Warranty

The author and publisher shall not be liable for your misuse of this material. This book is strictly for informational and educational purposes.

Warning – Disclaimer

The purpose of this book is to educate. The author and/or publisher do not guarantee that anyone following these techniques, suggestions, tips, ideas, or strategies will become successful. The author and/or publisher shall have neither liability nor responsibility to anyone with respect to any loss or damage caused, or alleged to be caused, directly or indirectly by the information contained in this book.

*To Peter, Annika, and Noah. You make it worthwhile. I am blessed to call you mine.*

Finally, brothers, whatever is true, whatever is noble, whatever is right, whatever is pure, whatever is lovely, whatever is admirable—if anything is excellent or praiseworthy—think about such things.

—Phillippians 4:8

# Table of Contents

Introduction ................................................................... ix
Playing it Safe Can Be Dangerous ........................................... 1
How Do You Define Success? ............................................... 11
Spend Your Energy Wisely .................................................. 21
A Room Full of Frauds ....................................................... 29
Asking for the Sale Doesn't Mean You're Pushy .................... 35
The Phone: Friend or Foe? .................................................. 45
Whose Job is it? ................................................................ 51
You Don't Need Motivation, You Need Momentum ............. 57
What to Do When You Know What to Do, But You Don't Feel Like Doing It .................................................. 63
Author's Note: My Secret Sauce ......................................... 69
Acknowledgements ............................................................ 73
About Deirdre .................................................................... 75

# Introduction

Let's face it. Promoting yourself, your skills, and your business can slam even the most confident of us up against a wall of fear and self-doubt. Let me ask you a question: Who is making your decisions for you?

Without even knowing it, you may have allowed fear to become the executive decision maker in your head. You wonder why you struggle with certain aspects of your business and personal life and yet you don't know what to do about it.

There is something you can do. You can let me show you how to fire fear from that role. Doing so will change the way you think so you can create the professional and personal life you dream about.

Through my own personal experience, coaching others and speaking to groups of professionals, I've learned that most business problems are really personal problems in disguise. They are the result of our having a particular mindset. How we see and think about things affects the decisions we make and the actions we take. To boil it down, your mindset is either your biggest asset or greatest hindrance. You can have all the skill, money, and connections in the world, but if you don't master your mindset so that you can navigate the rocky terrain of owning a business, your chances of success diminish substantially.

To my point, there was a study done a few years ago by businessman Fred Berni, owner of Dynamic Performance Systems, Inc., and a group of psychologists. For several years they surveyed hundreds of franchise owners to see if they could figure out what makes someone successful. The results were quite interesting. They found that attitude above all was the greatest predictor of future business success. Does this surprise you? This is great news! Your attitude—the way you perceive things and what you choose to do with those perceptions—is one of the only things in life you can control.[1]

Let me give you an example of a client of mine who, by changing her mindset, also changed her business and personal life. When Linda came to me for coaching, she was already a top sales person in her industry. Still, she wanted to work with me because she wanted to spend more time with her husband and three small children, and raise her business to the next level. During this time, I took her through a systematic process that uncovered, challenged, and changed the mindsets that were making her feel stuck and overwhelmed. For example, she thought that if she clearly stated her business hours her clients would think her incompetent and go somewhere else. She also thought that if she asked to be paid for a certain aspect of her job (where she really deserved to be paid), others would think she was greedy or pushy.

Because she changed her limiting mindsets about herself and her business she started to learn new skills and put new procedures in place. The results were amazing! Fourteen months after we started coaching, she increased her income by 65% percent during one of the worst economic recessions in history, created the focused time she wanted with her family, increased her self-confidence, and had greater job and life satisfaction.

If you are not yet convinced that having the right mindset is critical to your business success. Let me share a personal story with you.

The book you are holding in your hands is the book I was looking for many years ago, a book that would help me navigate the complicated and often terrifying path of a an entrepreneur. Let me explain.

In 2001, I made a decision that left me devastated. Two years prior I was bitten badly by the entrepreneurial bug. The promise of being in control of what I did and how I did it, plus

---

[1] Steve Strauss, "A successful franchise centers on attitude," USA Today, 7 July 2004, http://www.usatoday.com/money/smallbusiness/columnist/strauss/2004-07-11-franchise_x.htm (accessed October 27, 2010)

the dream of making unlimited income, drew me in like a bee to honey. For two years I poured my heart and soul into my health and wellness business, but felt like I was on one big emotional and mental roller coaster ride. If someone bought a product or liked what I was doing I was elated and confident, if someone refused to learn about or buy my product I felt defeated and succumbed to self-doubt.

After two years, I finally pulled the plug on this venture because I was exhausted. I couldn't take the roller coaster anymore. I realized that although I loved the *idea* of running my own business, I did not have the mindset needed to be successful. The relentless pursuit of bringing in business, the constant rejection, having to ask for the sale, and doing things I didn't like—such as paperwork and making follow up calls—when I had no one to make me do them was more than I could handle. My idealistic dream came tumbling down around me. I thought having my own business would give me power and control over my career. But because I kept crashing into my own limitations, instead I felt small and inferior.

I remember telling myself the day I quit that I was a failure. That thought devastated me perhaps the most because I had always been successful at whatever I'd set my mind to in the past. This time I felt like my mind was failing me. The really sad part is that I allowed that idea of myself, that I was a failure, to follow me around for many years, causing me a lot of pain and despair, paralyzing me from moving forward and stunting my ability to learn from this situation.

When I quit, I thought my desire to have my own business would go away but it didn't. So I started what I considered a safe business soon after: real estate investing. Now I know that's ironic because most people consider real estate investing a scary business on several levels, but for me it was safe. Here's why: I didn't have to depend on anyone else to make it successful. I didn't need clients so no chance of rejection; no awkward moments of asking for the sale. Plus, I loved the hunt of finding the perfect property, negotiating the purchase price and figuring out the financing so I was able to stay motivated and on task. For four years it seemed I had found the perfect business. But something was missing. I grew tired, lonely really, over the fact that I needed few others to be successful. I missed the human element. My safe business had grown lifeless and mechanical. I realized that while I was now an investor for life and would continue to manage the properties I had, it would not satisfy my daily need for fulfillment and human interaction. Being an investor had become a retirement strategy rather than a career. So, I decided I wanted to put myself out there again and start a business focused on helping people. This terrified me because I wasn't sure I could handle failure again, however, it felt like a part of me would never feel whole if I didn't at least try to make a go of it. Thanks to my first experience, I realized if I didn't learn how to develop a mindset that could withstand failure and rejection, I wouldn't make it in my next business either.

I knew I needed help thinking differently so I started looking for how-to books and stories of entrepreneurs who had previously-failed businesses and then went on to find success. I wanted them to tell me their secret, their formula. I couldn't find any. I wasn't sure where to turn to next when my cousin introduced me to her coach. I am sure it was no coincidence that her coach was a Certified Fearless Living Coach. Since I knew fear was at the center of my limited thinking I hired her immediately to help me. Little did I realize how profoundly God would use this experience as the catalyst for changing my attitude and how I approached both my personal and business life. That process, coupled with diving in and starting my own coaching and speaking business, changed me from someone who was stuck, afraid, and undisciplined to someone who now faces challenges head on, gets things done no matter what, and who has consistently grown her coaching and speaking business—in a down economy- since starting in 2007.

So there you have it. I wanted to tell you my story so you know that I get it. This is not a book filled with a bunch of theories written by someone on the outside looking in. Rather the principles are simple, practical, and, the best part is, they work.

This book contains some of the secrets I was hoping to find many years ago, and my prayer is that by reading it, you can start following a new path. A path that will enable you to get out of your own way and go after what you want in your business. The central goal of this book is to help you develop a new way of thinking, one that is resistant to failure, fear, and distractions. Once you do that you can get off the roller coaster ride of emotions that so often accompanies being an entrepreneur.

**How to use the book:**

The following pages contain the nine most common issues raised by my clients and audience members in regards to limited thinking. Each chapter discusses one of these limiting thoughts, gives examples, and provides an action step for you to take in order to change it. I encourage you to read through the book once before implementing the action steps. Then, go back and put each step in place one-by-one. Do not get overwhelmed by thinking you have to incorporate all of these points into your life at once. Pick the step that will give you the most bang for your buck and start there. When you're ready, begin practicing the next one and so on. Rest assured that if you incorporate just one or two of the ideas in this book, your business will begin to see growth.

Ready to get started? Let's go!

Avoiding danger is no safer in the long run than outright exposure. Life is either a daring adventure or nothing.

—Helen Keller

# Playing it Safe Can Be Dangerous

Many people believe that if something scares them they should back away from it. Actually, in most cases, the opposite is true. A few months ago, I ran into a client I worked with at the beginning of my career as a coach and speaker. She said to me, "So now that you've been doing this for a while, do you find that you're less fearful?" I thought for a few moments and replied, "I don't know if I'm less fearful. What I do know is that I recover much faster from fearful situations. I've also realized that if I'm not scared I'm not playing a big enough game." Wow. We looked at each other, both realizing how profound that statement was. I had never quite said it that way before, but it's true.

If you are not scared, you are not playing a big enough game. What kind of reaction do you have to that? When I say this to clients and audiences at speaking engagements they usually let out a nervous laugh before giving a collective nod followed by dead silence. It's the moment they realize it's true. Once you grasp this, the sky is the limit. Fear no longer has to equal disaster. No longer does it mean that because you feel afraid you will do a poor job. Rather it means you are entering new and exciting territory and that yes, you are on the right track. Remembering this truth helps me enormously in my daily life.

Here's a recent example: I had just gotten home from a meeting at the National Speakers Association Minnesota chapter (NSA MN). The NSA MN offers several year-long courses that speakers can take. Two of the courses seemed to be good options for me. One was a basic course called the Apprentice Program that focused on the fundamentals of becoming a speaker, and helping participants decide if this was the best profession for them. The other class called the

Graduate Program focused on digging deep and creating an active and viable speaking business. It seemed the Graduate Program was a better fit because I was already getting paid to speak, had already committed myself to growing this part of my business, yet I knew that I could also gain a lot from the Apprentice Program. I was not sure what to do.

I asked the instructors for their opinion. Two told me to take the Graduate Program, one said stick to the Apprentice Program—my original intent prior to going to the meeting that night. I started feeling anxious over not knowing the "right" answer, especially since I wanted to make my decision that night so that I wouldn't "over think" it in the days to come. I was leaning towards the Graduate Program but felt fear welling up inside me just thinking about it. All these "What if's?" came to the surface: "What if I'm not ready for that program?"; "What if I miss something essential by not taking the Apprentice Program?"; "What if by taking the Graduate Program I'm thinking I'm better than I really am?" On the flip side, thinking about the Apprentice Program brought up no emotion whatsoever. I thought, "Wow, that would be really easy to do."

When I had that thought, I knew what my decision was going to be. I signed up for the Graduate Program. I thought about how fear was an indication of my need to play a bigger game. I realized that even though I was scared I was excited too!

One of my life principles is to challenge myself. I knew if I took the other course I would be letting myself off the hook by taking the easy way out. The next morning I woke up feeling more excited to get out of bed than usual. This excitement confirmed that I made the right decision. Was I still a bit scared? Yes, but facing my fears head-on and choosing to grow versus back away has the power to make you feel more alive. It's the same reason many of us enjoy roller coasters. They scare us, and yet at the same time we find that they are an exhilarating reminder that we're alive.

When building a business there is no room for playing it safe. If you want to have the business you dream about, you will have to do things that scare you. For many years, before becoming a coach and speaker, I played it safe. When I was selling wellness products, I was afraid if I asked for someone's business I was being pushy and making them uncomfortable. So I rarely asked. The result? A struggling business and a major hit to my self-esteem. Looking back I know that, truthfully, I was the one who was uncomfortable and assumed, based on my own feelings, that my potential customer was too. What I've learned is that my success or lack of it largely depends on my willingness to be uncomfortable.

See, most of us wait until we feel confident before we move forward with a certain task. We reason that we're not ready yet, we need a little longer, and somehow, by waiting, voilà!, we are finally confident and ready to move forward. This whole line of thinking is backwards. It's action, repeated action, actually doing things that scare us that grows our confidence, not the other way around.

Take my client Valerie, for example. Valerie is an attorney who was afraid to give her clients a definitive answer on what they should do in certain cases. Instead of giving them her opinion on the best course of action, she would give her clients several options and ask them to decide. Why? She was afraid they'd think she had an agenda, especially if she advised them to choose the more expensive option. The result to her practice? Many of her clients chose to do nothing. Valerie recognized her fear of advising as a mindset she wanted—needed—to change. In order to do that she had to face her fear head on and actually start seeing herself as an authority who had their best interest at heart.

The first few times she gave her direct opinions she was really scared. Over time, though, it became less scary and more natural. These days she finds her clients listen to and appreciate her advice. Few clients choose to do nothing. With her guidance they choose a direction and follow it. Valerie is thrilled because her clients are getting something they really need and she is building her practice and her confidence.

On that note, let's talk about confidence. I believe confidence is a shaky foundation on which to build your dreams. Now I like confidence as much as the next gal, in fact it's my preferred way of feeling, but I have learned over the years that it's unreliable, and I am not willing to stake my future on something unreliable. Through my own experience as well as encouraging, challenging, and observing my clients, I have realized there is a quality we all have access to that is much more reliable than confidence. A quality that will stand firm as a foundation for you to build your business. Want to know what it is?

It's courage. It takes courage to continue to move forward when you are afraid. You do not need confidence to be successful, you need courage. Keep taking steps relying on courage and eventually more confidence will come. Do this over and over, as a way of life, and your comfort zone will expand in ways you never thought possible. Things that used to terrify me a few years ago now feel as easy as brushing my teeth. That's because I acted with courage, over and over again.

Think about a toddler learning to walk. Then imagine if he said to himself, "Gee, I think I'll wait until I know I can do this, yes that sounds good, maybe I'll read a book about walking first and then ask a few of my friends what they think. Then I'll take that first step." If toddlers did that, we'd be a world full of crawlers. It took courage, not confidence, for each toddler to take that first step.

## Action Steps

1) Write down something you've avoided doing in your business, an action that scares you, but you know would help move you forward. Then break that task in several small, very small if needed, steps. Next to each step ask yourself on a scale of 0-10 how much that task scares you (0 being "This is so easy," 10 being "There is no way I am doing that"). Next put either a start or an end date next to each step. Begin with the least scary task, then work your way up to the scariest.

Here's an example of one of mine:

Write a book on how to grow your business by changing the way you think.

1.) Start writing 6; 3/15/2010

2.) Tell people about it 9; 6/1/2010

3.) Hire someone to type and edit it 7; 4/1/2010

4.) Buy a nice journal that I will enjoy writing in 3; 3/15/2010

5.) Buy a great pen 3; 3/15/2010

6.) Give myself a completion deadline 9; 11/1/2010

7.) Put money into layout and design 10; 10/1/2010

You'll notice I have two three's, a six, a seven, two nine's and a ten. I chose to work on the lower numbers first, gaining the confidence to tackle the higher numbers. You can do this, too.

2) The other piece to living outside your comfort zone is to make a plan to support your self. It is really hard, and frankly unnecessary, to rely only on yourself when facing your fears. Decide what kind of support will help you accomplish the tasks you've listed. Support comes in many forms: getting a coach, other people, prayer, Bible study, writing a script, exercising, getting a massage, healthy eating, etc. Whatever support will help you increase your courage and your well being, be sure to incorporate it into your life. For example, the first time

I did a paid speaking engagement I was really scared. I asked my best friend to be in the audience for support.

3) Lastly, most of us make decisions by asking ourselves if we are comfortable doing a certain thing. Like I said in the introduction, that's fear being your executive decision maker. Don't do this. Instead, I encourage you to have a life philosophy that challenges you to do things that scare you. Like my example with the NSA MN, instead of going in the opposite direction or doing nothing when you feel afraid, move towards the thing you're scared of. If you do you will find yourself leading a life of excitement, one where you live up to your potential. The best part is you will feel, perhaps for the first time, truly alive.

**Notes**

A life spent making mistakes is not only more honorable, but more useful than a life spent in doing nothing.

—George Bernard Shaw

# How Do You Define Success?

Your definitions of success and failure are critical to your ability to promote yourself for the long haul. If you view success as making a sale or bringing in a new client, and failure as anything but that, you will ride a constant roller coaster of emotions that may lead to burn out. As one of my clients put it, "I'm always failing until I hit my goal." See, our lives are generally not made up of big moments. Of course we all experience several big moments like getting married or having children, bringing in that dream client or getting a promotion. But the fabric of our lives is mostly sewn together with small decisions, many small decisions, made throughout a day. This is why in order to feel good about yourself and your business on a daily basis, your definition of success must include celebrating the little victories, the small steps along the way that will lead to the big moments.

For example, for the first two years of my speaking and coaching practice my definition of success was about reaching a certain level of production. It didn't matter that I was helping people change their lives. I never allowed myself to feel successful until I reached my monthly goal for bringing in clients. Eventually I got to a point where I was tired of being dissatisfied with my self and my business. Interestingly, I typically did hit my production goals but the journey to get there was tumultuous. I only got to enjoy success once a month, the day I hit my monthly goal.

I spent those two years plus many years prior in my other businesses asking business owners this question: How do you hold on to your production or financial goals, keep working towards them and yet still are able to relax and find contentment along the way? No one, least of all me, knew the answer to this. It seemed like either I focused on my goals, thus feeling discontent and anxious until I hit them (not a way to live life), or I forgot about my goals and just took things as they came (not a way to run a business). Neither option appealed to me. So I started to pray about it—something I should have done first, perhaps saving myself years of searching—and received the answer I was looking for. It was my definition of success that was the problem. I had to change my definition of success in order to go after my goals and still feel successful and content while doing it. As long as my definition was about the end result rather than the process I went through to get there, I would never be satisfied. This is a life-changing idea. Success has to be found in the process, not the results for two reasons: 1) You can control how you approach the process, but you cannot control the results; 2) If your self-worth is wrapped up in achieving your goals you will never be content.

I realized I had to create a way to enjoy and celebrate success every day. To do that my definition could not center around numbers. I let this idea percolate for a few days. I thought about what value I wanted to bring to the world. When I left this earth, what did I want people to say I contributed? I decided to build my new definition of success around that.

Here's what I came up with. Success for me is:

1.) Serving God by using the gifts He has given me.
2.) Connecting with others and being a positive force in their lives.
3.) Doing things that scare me and will challenge me to grow.

Compare that with the type of definition I had been using in my business life for years:

1.) Enroll eight clients for a Get Clients Now!™ class
2.) Book a speaking engagement
3.) Write a book

Can you see the difference? Do you notice how my old definition is really a series of goals? My old definition only focused on results whereas my new one focuses on my values and the process of moving forward to achieve my goals? I still have monthly "production" goals, if you will, but once I set them I put them aside so I can focus on the journey of hitting my goals. I touched on this already but it bears repeating; I believe written goals and goals said aloud to others are critical to growing your business, but they should **never** be part of your definition of success. Why? Again, because then your self-worth as a person is determined by whether or not you hit those goals. That is a losing proposition.

In contrast, when your definition of success focuses on the journey, you are able to celebrate victory every step of the way. For example, when I hit just one of my three criteria I am successful. Every time I push myself to do something that scares me I celebrate my success; when I have clearly helped someone else I celebrate my success, etc.

Here's a specific instance: a woman who heard me speak said she wanted to have a private coaching consultation with me. We emailed back and forth a few times, trying to find a mutual time that worked. We couldn't find one and she finally told me she really needed an evening appointment. "Uh-oh," I thought, "now I have a decision to make." A long time ago, I decided that in order to protect my family time I would not schedule evening coaching clients. Up until then, no one had ever asked to meet in the evening. I was conflicted inside because on one hand I wanted a new private client and I thought she and I would be a good fit. On the other hand I wanted to honor the boundaries I had set for my personal life. My fear was saying if I didn't do it a future client might walk away. The other side of me, the side that wanted to make a choice driven by my own free will and not fear, said that I needed to get out of my comfort zone, tell this woman I don't hold evening appointments, and if she walks away she does. She'll find someone else to help her and there will always be more clients. I followed this voice and my potential client did walk away.

The next day I was dwelling on this and second-guessing myself. I wondered if I should I have said okay to an evening session. Could I have said things differently so she would have made a daytime session work? And on it went. I started feeling worse and worse before I realized that I was telling myself I was a failure. Thankfully, halfway through the day, I remembered my new definition of success and decided to run this situation through that lens versus the lens of my old definition, which is what I had been doing. I went down the list of my three ingredients for success, and realized in this situation I had done something that scared me and I had challenged myself to grow. I was elated! This meant that instead of telling myself I was a failure because I lost a potential client, I was actually successful according to my new definition. This was a huge moment for me. I still felt a bit sad, but I was able to stop the negative thoughts that were trying to convince me I was a failure. Do you see how powerful this is?

Rather than celebrating only once—when I bring in new business—I get to celebrate all the steps it took to bring in the new business. The ironic part is that focusing on the journey helps me achieve my financial goals more consistently than focusing on the financial goals alone. It's ironic but not surprising. Can you see how if I focus on serving God by using my gifts, connecting with others, and doing things that scare me how much easier it is to reach my goals? The best part is I have a lot of fun and experience a lot of fulfillment along the way.

## Action Steps

1) Write down your current definition of success. Be really specific. Often my clients tell me they want to be successful yet when I ask them what that means they don't know. When my clients finally figure it out they can see why they feel as though they're always running in circles around a hamster wheel. Most business owners define success as hitting production numbers. If this is your measuring stick anxiety, overwhelm, and desperation can easily set in.

2) Once you've written down your current definition, write a new definition that portrays how you want to show up in the world as a person, and the value you want to bring to others as you strive to hit your goals. Think about how you want to deliver your service, what type of person you want to be in your business relationships, and what you can contribute to this world. Put your new definition of success in a place where you will see it every day throughout the day so you can internalize it. Internalizing your definition will take time and practice but it's worth it. At the end of each day write down the ways in which you succeeded using your new definition as your measuring stick. Make a point to recognize and celebrate the "small" victories. Don't skip this step. This will help your new definition really become yours. The more you internalize it, the less overwhelmed and anxious you will feel and the more peace, satisfaction, and excitement you will add to your life. Lastly, make a point to start judging your success through this lens, recognizing and celebrating the "small" victories.

Now let's talk about failure. Fear of failure is one of the most common things that hold people back. For many people this fear can be absolutely paralyzing. Author and speaker John Maxwell is an authority on success and leadership. In his book *Failing Forward* he says, "The only difference between average people and achieving people is their perception of and response to failure. Nothing else has the same kind of impact on people's ability to achieve and to accomplish whatever their minds and hearts desire." Wow! That is a bold and exciting statement. It means that no matter what's happened in your life up until now, you can change your mindset and achieve what you want. The question Maxwell says to ask is this: "If you looked at failure and responded to failure differently than you do now, what would you attempt to achieve?"[2]

1) Write down your definition of failure. Be honest with yourself. You have to know what you really think in order to challenge that belief.

2) Next, write a new definition, one that will support you as you begin to pick yourself up and move forward when you get knocked down. For example, one of my clients used to believe that making a mistake, any mistake, equaled failure. Now, her new perception is that failures are stepping stones to success. I love that definition and have adopted it as my own. Which belief do you think will serve her better? Obviously the new one.

3) Lastly, write a list of all the things you've avoided doing because you were afraid to fail. Look at them through the lens of your new perception and see how your response to doing those things could now be different. Make an action plan today to move toward the tasks and goals on your list using your new definitions of success and failure as your guides.

---

[2] John C. Maxwell, Failing Forward (Nashville: Thomas Nelson Publishers, 2000), 2

# Notes

If you don't like something change it; if you can't change it, change the way you think about it.

—Mary Engelbreit

# Spend Your Energy Wisely

We all wake up each day with a finite amount of what I call energy units. Energy units are the amount of energy you have to manage the events in your day in a positive and proactive manner. The amount each of us has depends on many factors: your personality, your mental health, your physical health, your spiritual health, and the actual events going on in your life. When you spend time dwelling on the negative you actually lose energy units that you could spend on creating opportunity and moving forward in your life.

I had never thought of energy this way until a few years ago. My kids were acting up one night before bed and when I started actually putting them in their beds they each wanted me to spend time with them before they went to sleep. I remember looking at my daughter, saying, "I have no energy left for that right now because I used up all my energy when you and your brother weren't listening to me." It was the first time I realized my energy is finite and my capacity for handling things in a positive manner depends at least partly on how many units I give away to difficult, annoying, frustrating situations.

Now I am not suggesting we stuff our feelings and pretend all is perfect. Most of us will face some very difficult if not devastating things in our lifetime, and we should allow ourselves to grieve and process the emotions that come with that. What we can avoid is spending excessive energy dwelling on the things that anger or frustrate us, thus saving energy units for creating and responding to more of what we want in our lives.

Let me give you an example of what I mean. A few months ago I was driving to a meeting with an organization that was interested in hiring me to work with their students.

Right before I left I had received a message from a prospect who had decided not to work with me. I started to dwell on this. I realized the more I dwelled, the more self-doubt crept in. I started wondering if I was really a "good enough" coach. Fortunately, I quickly realized what I was doing. The energy I spent indulging my negative thoughts was taking away from the energy I needed, energy I wanted to have for my upcoming meeting. I realized the past was done, that the prospect had already said no, but the future was still up for grabs. Did I really want to lessen my chances of being hired by this organization because I was off my game? All because I decided to dwell on something negative that I couldn't change anyway?

Since that day I manage my energy very carefully. Like anyone, I get mad, sad, disappointed, and frustrated by things in my life and business, but now when things come up I realize I am making a choice. I can dwell in the negative (and once in a while I choose to) and have less energy or I can decide I don't want to waste energy units and move on.

## Action Steps

Create an "energy audit."

1) First make a list of all the people, situations, or things that you are "putting up with." This area of energy drain is often overlooked. It's the things in our physical environment that bother us daily but that we tell ourselves, "Oh it's no big deal I'll just put up with that. For example, I have lived in my house for six years and have never hung my full-length mirror on the wall. Every morning I have to prop it up on a garbage can in my room to get a full-body view. Every morning this annoys me (not a great way to start a day), and every morning I "put up with it." Likewise, I have a client whose house is so cluttered that it makes it hard for her to focus at work (even though she does not work from home). For you it may be the messy desk or the doorbell that doesn't work. This may seem trite but add up all the things you put up with and it can be a major drain on your energy units.

Go through your physical environment (house, work, car) and write down all the things that bug you. Next, rank them in order of most to least draining. Make an action plan to correct these items. Once you do, you'll be surprised at how much energy you added to your day.

2) Make a list of all the people/situations/things that give you energy and be sure to incorporate a few of those into each day. For example, if I have a day scheduled for paperwork (drains energy) I make sure I meet with someone for coffee or go work out (gives me energy).

3) When you find yourself indulging in negative thoughts, cut it off and focus on something positive. Remember energy is like compounding interest. The more positive energy you have the more you'll get, the more negative energy you have the more you'll get of that.

4) Pick a time of day—ideally the same time each day—when you allow yourself to journal, write, or talk out loud

about all the things that bug you. Set a timer anywhere between 5-15 minutes. During this time you get to be as negative as you need to be. Once the timer goes off, you're done for the day. This is a great way to contain negative energy while at the same time allowing yourself to express your emotions.

# Notes

A man would do nothing if he waited until he could do it so well that no one would find fault.

—John Henry Newman

# A Room Full of Frauds

One of the common themes that come up with my private clients is that they are worried they are not good enough. They are afraid that at any moment the other shoe is going to drop and that people will find out "the truth" about them. What's "the truth?" That they have tricked people into believing they know what they're doing, but really they don't. That they are, in fact, a fraud.

Does this sound familiar? If so, I have good news. You may think this is your shameful little secret but you are not alone. Not by a long shot. This way of feeling and thinking is so common among successful professionals it even has a name. It's known as The Imposter Syndrome and if you feel this way you know it really holds you back from going after what you want and living up to your fullest potential.

Wikipedia defines the Imposter Syndrome as this:

> The impostor syndrome, sometimes called impostor phenomenon or fraud syndrome, is a psychological phenomenon in which people are unable to internalize their accomplishments . . . . Regardless of what level of success they may have achieved in their chosen field of work or study or what external proof they may have of their competence, those with the syndrome remain convinced internally they do not deserve the success they have achieved and are actually frauds. Proof of success is dismissed as luck, timing, or as a result of deceiving others into

thinking they were more intelligent and competent than they believe themselves to be.[3]

What you need to know is that you are not a fraud. You only feel that way.

I am going to get out of my comfort zone by telling you that I felt that way for years. I would be sitting in a meeting and all of a sudden I would imagine myself shrinking and my chair expanding. I would feel like I was this little girl in a huge chair, waiting for someone to "find out" there was a child in the room and that she did not belong there.

This prevented me from accomplishing goals that were really important to me. When I finally found out that there was a name for this and that many other people, especially successful ones, had the same fears I could have cried for joy. The relief I felt was huge. I realized that if so many other successful people, people I looked up to, felt the same way it couldn't be true. It was only the way I felt, not reality!

Just knowing that released some of the hold this way of thinking had on me. These days that feeling will rear its ugly head once in a while. But because of the work I've done with my coach and even helping my clients with this, I don't buy into it and am able to recognize this as fear giving me the wrong information. Take it from me, when you let go of this fear a whole new world of possibilities will open up for you.

---

[3] Wikipedia contributors," Impostor Syndrome," Wikipedia, The Free Encyclopedia, http://en.wikipedia.org/wiki/Impostor_syndrome#References (accessed October 22, 2010)

**Action Steps**

1) If you can identify with what I've said, the next time those feelings and thoughts come up, look around you. You are not the only person who feels out of their element. We all do a good job of wearing our game face, but I guarantee you there are several if not many people in the room who feel the exact same way. Can it be true for all of you? I don't think so.

2) Tell yourself that just because you feel or think something does not make it true. In this case choose to believe other people's positive feedback about your competence and success versus your own incorrect negative beliefs. In reality, it's very difficult to fool people into believing you are smart or competent. If they think that it's because it's true. At times, the Imposter Syndrome still comes up for me when I engage in business activities that are unfamiliar or really scary to me. My satirical voice comes out and says, "Deirdre, if you were really as good at this as others think then you'd already know this or already be good at this." What I've realized is that is not true.

3) Don't have an all-or-nothing attitude. Just because there's more for you to learn (there hopefully always will be) or because you're scared does not mean you are not capable and smart. One does not cancel out the other. You can be fabulous at your work and still be scared or not know how to do some parts of it.

4) Push forward in spite of the feelings and go after what you want. The more you do that the more confidence you will have and the less hold The Imposter Syndrome will have over you.

## Notes

I don't care how much power, brilliance, or energy you have, if you don't harness it and focus it on a specific target and hold it there you're never going to accomplish as much as your ability warrants.

—Zig Ziglar

# Asking for the Sale Doesn't Mean You're Pushy

I was on the phone with a prospective client who called me because she needed help learning how to be more assertive about bringing in business. This was an accomplished Attorney who, after I asked what she thought was holding her back, said, "I don't want to be pushy." Ah, yes, I thought—for my female clients in particular—it always comes down to that. I understood what she meant; I don't want to be pushy either.

Let me take you back ten years. I am sitting at a table with two prospective customers and my manager. I was selling wellness products at the time and was scared to death about being perceived as pushy. I had a sales goal I needed to hit by the last day of the month in order to qualify for company recognition and an increased commission level. This was the second to last day of the month and we had just spent two hours, plus several weeks worth of work, building a relationship with and educating Mr. and Mrs. Prospect on why they should purchase the system we were selling. Towards the end of the meeting they agree they'd like to buy $5000 worth of product. I was thrilled! They were making a significant investment in their health and I was getting a raise.

What happened next is one of the reasons I decided to leave that business and one of the reasons I knew if I ever had my own business again I'd have to change my mindset. Mr. Prospect looked at me and said, "Deirdre I'd rather buy this in a few days [for some reason that was better for them financially], but if it will help you [he understood sales and realized there was only one selling day left in the month] we will buy today." You're probably thinking, "Wow! What an amazing customer." And he was. Ready for my response?

"Oh no!" I said, "That's alright, it makes no difference to me either way." The look on my manager's face was a mix of shock, anger, and perhaps a hint of "I'm going to strangle you!" The truth was it mattered a lot! But because I didn't want to be perceived as pushy, I had just undone several weeks worth of work towards a very important deadline, and possibly robbed my customer out of better health sooner.

Looking back now it seems unimaginable that I said no to their offer because I didn't want to push them. But despite the fact that *they* offered to buy that day, that it was actually *their* idea, I thought if I said yes to their offer, I was making them do something they did not want to do.

All day long I work with clients who worry that they're going to be pushy so they do something like I did, or they do nothing. Here are the steps I use with my clients to break through the "I don't want to be pushy" mindset:

1) Relax. If you are worried about being pushy chances are good that you are not pushy and never will be. The qualities we worry about being are generally the ones we do anything to avoid being. So the fact that you're worried tells me you're not pushy. The problem is you have to bring in business and to do that you have to ask probing questions. And ask for the sale. This will feel pushy especially at first but it's not pushy. It's called doing business.

2) One of the big reasons you're afraid to ask for what you want is because you see the words "pushy" and "salesperson" as synonymous. If you're like most people you have an image of the used car salesman. You don't want to be like him so you avoid any activity that a salesperson may do. There are several levels between acting like a pushy used car salesman and doing nothing. Pushy and salesperson do not mean the same thing. This is an important limiting belief to move beyond. If you are a service professional (such as an Attorney, CPA, Financial Advisor, Consultant, Health Practitioner, etc.) what you

may not realize is that if you work for yourself or for a company that requires you to bring in business you are also a salesperson! The sooner you can embrace that rather than avoid it, the better off you'll be. It's important to realize that you can be a great salesperson and not be pushy.

## Action Step

Take out a piece of paper. Draw a vertical line down the center. On one side write the words "Pushy salesperson" as a header; on the other write "Me as a salesperson." Now write all the characteristics of that pushy salesperson. Think of one you've encountered to help you get ideas. Now think of a business or salesperson you liked and found helpful. Write down the characteristics of that person. My guess is that those lists are vastly different. You get to decide how to conduct yourself as a salesperson. There's no rule that you have to do it a certain way.

For example, one of my clients, Susan, wanted to start her own seminar business. The problem was she didn't want to be seen as a "salesperson." Through our coaching sessions, we discovered she thought being a salesperson meant being pushy, and she associated the word "pushy" with selling things to people that they didn't want and not taking "no" for an answer. Can you see her challenge? If Susan has to sell herself and her services to have a successful business, but defines a salesperson as the qualities listed above, her dream of having a seminar business is doomed. "The solution," I told her, "is to reframe how you define 'salesperson.'"

Susan knew she enjoyed helping people. She liked it when she found a need she could fulfill. From this knowledge, she decided that as a salesperson her primary objective would be to ask questions and listen for a need she could fulfill. Once she did this she would then ask for the sale. Rather than focusing on "selling" something, her mindset would be that she was looking for an opportunity to "serve." This made a big difference for Susan because it alleviated the pressure to be someone she did not want to be.

It's important to note that even armed with your new salesperson definition, in the beginning you may feel like you're still being pushy. You're not. There are three truths I want you to hold on to as you practice asking for business or referrals:

1) Every business owner has to be willing to ask for the sale. That's not being pushy, that's called staying in business.

2) Often times our feelings do not accurately portray reality. If you are someone who avoids asking for what you want it will feel pushy even when it's not.

3) Many times people are afraid to ask for business or a referral because they erroneously assume they are making the other person uncomfortable. The thought of making another person uncomfortable makes us uncomfortable and holds us back from asking.

4) Here's what I believe is true: You are responsible for how you treat people. For being respectful of others. You are not responsible for their response or for whether or not your asking for business makes them uncomfortable. That's their responsibility. Please let this truth sink in. This is no small realization. For years, I held myself back because I felt responsible for how someone felt or reacted. Remember my sales story at the beginning of this chapter? I didn't take my prospect's offer to buy right then because I thought I was responsible if they felt uncomfortable. I now know that I was confused.

See, we are responsible to people, not for people. Being responsible to people means treating others with respect and living up to what you promise them. Being responsible for them means trying to fix or control their emotional reactions to things. This is an exercise in futility. I think most of us struggle with this concept. The following way of thinking has freed me and countless others to really pursue serving people and the only way in business to really serve is to ask a prospect if you can serve them (i.e. asking for the sale).

Start assuming that we're all adults. What I mean by that is rest comfortably in the idea that as adults we can each handle and are responsible for our emotional responses. Assume that when a client or prospect says "yes" they mean it. Assume that when someone says, "I'm busy now but call me in two weeks," they really want you to call them. Take people at their word. If someone asks you to call them in two weeks because they are scared to tell you no, that's their job to figure out how to say no to people. It's not your job to try and figure out if their "yes" or "maybe" really means "no."

Like all the other action steps in this book, when you start practicing this it may feel scary and uncomfortable. Don't worry, you'll get used to it. This shift in thinking has been one of the main factors in my being able to consistently grow my business month by month. I'd be surprised if it doesn't become one of yours too.

**Notes**

Everyone is entitled to their own opinion, but not their own facts.

—Daniel Patrick Moynihan

# The Phone: Friend or Foe?

I was working with a client today when she mentioned the eighty-pound phone. Do you know what she's talking about? If you've ever looked for a job or made a sales call the eighty-pound phone may be very familiar to you. If you are wondering what I mean, the eighty-pound phone is a phenomenon that happens when we need to make a phone call we do not want to make. Suddenly this very friendly, often one-pound or less, device turns into a big eighty-pound man-eating giant!

This got me thinking, is it the phone, or is something else going on? The answer lies in what you tell yourself when you think about making calls. Are you telling yourself that you're probably bugging the person, that they really don't want to hear from you, and that you'll probably stumble over your words? Or are you saying that this person may need what you have to offer, will be excited to hear from you, and who cares if you say it perfectly, just be passionate about your message?

I had this conversation with a client just yesterday. He is a health professional who was making calls to businesses to see if he could come in and give a wellness presentation to employees. He was really intimidated by making the calls. I asked him what he was telling himself before he called. He said he thought he needed to sell himself to the person on the other end and therefore needed to say things perfectly. I said, "No wonder you're scared. What is a different message you can give yourself to make this easier?" He decided if he focused on finding out if they were interested in getting his help, rather than trying to sell them on why they should bring him in, it would be less scary. Plus he could speak from the heart as opposed to making sure he said it all perfectly. With that realization I could hear the relief in his voice. From follow up coaching sessions I know he has made a lot more calls since then.

Becoming aware of the messages you tell yourself about making calls, really about doing anything, is critical to your business success. You must work diligently at replacing the negative messages with positive ones. One of my mentors, Rhonda Britten, founder of The Fearless Living Institute, has a great question you can ask yourself when you succumb to negative thoughts: "Am I making this up or is it true?" Let's face it, often when we tell ourselves what others are thinking we are making it up! The only way you can know for sure is by asking the other person.

I think it's fascinating that I have yet to meet someone who makes up good things others are thinking about them. As Rhonda would say, "If you're going to make it up, make it up in your favor!"

Finally, focus on the part you can control, which is making the call and how you deliver your message. Realize that you cannot control how the person on the other line is going to receive you. An amazing thing happens when you start to focus on the process (making the call) and give yourself credit for what you can control: the results over time take care of themselves.

**Action Steps**

1) Before you make calls tune in to your self-talk. If it's negative shift to positive messages. Even if at first you don't believe those messages, they will help!

2) Recognize that you are making things up! You have no idea what the recipient's reaction will be.

3) Worrying will not help you control the outcome. You cannot control the outcome. The only thing you can control is whether you make the call and what your attitude is. Focus on those two things.

4) Again, no matter the outcome celebrate the fact that you made the call. When you start to focus on the process (making the call) and give yourself credit for that, over time the phone will turn back into the one-pound device it was meant to be.

## Notes

Nothing is so often irretrievably missed as a daily opportunity.

—Marie Von Ebner-Eschenbach

## Whose Job is it?

One summer, I was working with a client who is a very talented photographer and speaker. Like many entrepreneurs she has something of high value to offer, but was tentative when it came to prospecting and follow up. Her reason? She didn't want to pester people, and thought if people were interested in her service they'd call her. I told her the truth, "It's not your client's job to mind your business. It's your job." She looked at me like, "Huh?" But all of a sudden I saw the light bulb going off. She was having an a-ha moment.

See, all too often we get confused about who does what. We expect that if someone is really interested in our services they will follow up with us. We expect that if they wanted our service or product they would be thinking about us as often as we think about them. Never mind that they have their own lives and businesses to care for. These assumptions are wrong and often hold us back when we should move forward.

I am not telling you to pester people. I am encouraging you to stay in the forefront of the minds of interested prospects so that when they're ready to buy you're there. Do yourself a huge favor and stop expecting your clients to do the follow-up work for you. How often have you dropped an interested prospect after only one or two attempts at touching base with them? You've probably assumed they didn't really want to talk to you. In reality, studies show it takes between five and twelve touches with a prospect before they buy.

How about trusting their word? If they said they want to talk with you believe that they do until they tell you otherwise. We live in a culture of instant gratification and want results now! When we don't get them we think we'll never get them and move on. Now, we should move on from some people but I am not talking about them. I am talking about the ones who have expressed a genuine interest in your product or service, but you have yet to touch base with them or they have decided not to buy at this time. Continue to follow up with them until they say otherwise.

One thing I do that has really helped me with follow up is to ask their permission to follow up again. I'll say something such as, "If I don't here from you in two weeks, may I follow up with you again?" They typically say yes. This really helps me because then I don't have to worry about being a pest; they've given me permission to contact them again. A word of caution: if you ask that question and get permission, make sure you do in fact follow up or your credibility will diminish in your prospect's eyes. They won't be thinking about you every day, but if weeks or months go by and you have not made contact they will notice.

**Action Step**

What would you do differently if you started looking at your business from this point of view: "It's my job to mind my own business not my prospect's or my client's"? Stop what you're doing, close your eyes and really think about the answer to this question. Now write your answer down.

I believe the answer has the power to transform your business. It has for my client. She is now proactive in her follow up, and takes herself more seriously. She realizes she has something valuable to offer her clients and the only way they'll know that is if she follows up with them. She now takes people at their word and when they ask her to follow up at a later date she does. Because she now believes people really want to talk to her, she no longer feels like she is begging for work or that the prospect is doing her a favor by talking to her. The result? Increased income, more opportunity, and greater self-confidence.

**Notes**

Action is the anecdote to despair.

—Joan Baez

# You Don't Need Motivation, You Need Momentum

Waiting for motivation is a business and self-confidence killer. Let me give you an example: My client, Tom, called me one morning for our session and said glumly, "I didn't get much done this week, I guess what I need is to get motivated." I responded with "You don't need motivation, you need momentum!"

See, you don't ever want to wait until you're motivated to do something. That sounds counterintuitive but it's true. Many of us wrongly believe that motivation is the fuel that gets us moving. It's not. It's the byproduct of getting into action. Does that surprise you? It did me. I learned this truth about 20 years ago and was shocked when I first heard it. At that time I had spent days, weeks, even years waiting to get motivated to do something. I thought if I waited long enough motivation would eventually come. When it didn't I used that as a good reason to beat myself up and tell myself I was lazy, a loser, a procrastinator, and in a word (alright three words really) "not good enough." Surely someone more competent would be better able to get things done.

The truth is that action, taking action, is what gets us moving. Action is the fuel; motivation is the byproduct. When you start taking action towards getting something done you build momentum. It's the momentum that will give you the motivation you've been desperately searching for. Remember this equation: Action + Action + Action = Momentum = Motivation.

Back to my client, Tom. His lack of action in the name of waiting for motivation caused him to lose a week of time growing his business, and was a major blow to his self-esteem.

Once Tom understood how motivation works he made a commitment to himself that he was going to take action whether he felt motivated or not. Tom described this realization and commitment to action as the big breakthrough his mindset needed in order to build the business of his dreams.

Four weeks after Tom had this mindset shift he started hitting 100 percent of his weekly goal. Within eight weeks he went from being concerned about making his business work from a cash flow perspective to no longer worrying about paying his overhead. This was a huge accomplishment! Because Tom now relies on action and momentum versus motivation, he is consistently hitting his goals and making his practice more profitable week by week.

## Action Steps

1) What is something you have been unmotivated to do? Make a list of three actions you can take today towards getting it done. The actions do not have to be big. Small actions are great because they're easy to do and start to build on each other giving you the momentum you need to complete the task.

2) Use a timer. If you find it's really difficult to start a task, set a timer for five, ten, or fifteen minutes. Get started on the task and once the timer goes off you're done. I've used this technique often. It gets me moving and builds momentum so that when the timer goes off I usually reset it for more time. Plus I feel really good about accomplishing something I didn't want to do.

3) Don't beat yourself up for not being motivated for what you haven't done. Instead, give yourself kudos for the actions you took no matter how small. This attitude towards yourself will help you move forward. In fact, that's how I am getting this chapter done right now!

## Notes

You cannot make yourself feel something you do not feel, but you can make yourself do right in spite of your feelings.

—Pearl S. Buck

# What to Do When You Know What to Do, But You Don't Feel Like Doing It

This chapter is going to include a healthy dose of tough love. It comes from the place in me that cares deeply about you fulfilling your purpose here on earth. As a business owner, you have to be willing to train your will. If you are not willing to do things you do not feel like doing, don't expect your business to be successful. I've got news for you. Not enjoying something or not feeling like doing something is not a valid reason for low performance. Ouch. If it helps, you're not alone. This is something I work with my clients on all the time.

One of the principles I live by is that my "not enjoying" something is not a good enough reason not to do it, if doing it serves a higher goal. This principle has changed me from someone who, ten years ago, was very undisciplined when working for myself, hence a failed business, to now being someone who gets things done no matter what I feel about it. This mindset is key to running my two successful businesses.

Let me give you an example of how you can put this idea into action. One of my clients, we'll call him Ron, came to me because he knew what wanted to do to grow his business, he just wasn't doing it. During our coaching sessions, we figured out he wasn't doing certain key tasks because he didn't "like" them. Because he didn't like them, he never "felt" like doing them. He really thought this was a valid reason, that he was justified in not getting these tasks done. We talked about the principle of not letting your feelings decide your behavior. I asked him to write down what he would get from doing the disliked tasks. This is what he came up with:

1) Increased income
2) Feel productive
3) Increased satisfaction
4) My boss would no longer bug me

When looking at his list, he realized that what he gained in the end from doing them was huge. He decided instead of continually letting himself off the hook by giving in to his feelings, he was going to focus on the underlying values doing those things brought him. His mantra became "I am willing to do the things I don't like because it makes me money." With this mantra in mind, he now consistently does the previously dreaded tasks. He also now sees how doing these actions helps him achieve his goal of becoming a trusted advisor to his clients. After just a few weeks of coaching with me and applying this principle to his work he is more productive, is hitting his goals, and feels better about himself. In fact he told me that the tasks he didn't like to do before, the ones he avoided, no longer annoy him. They have become a habit, just a regular part of his day. As an added bonus, his superiors have noticed a shift too!

## Action Steps

1) What is one thing you don't feel like doing that if you do it would make a difference in your business? Recognize that not "feeling like" doing something is an excuse and not a good one at that. Commit right now to stop making excuses, stop letting yourself off the hook. Stop allowing "I don't feel like it" make your decisions for you. Like Ron, make a list of the benefits you receive from doing those tasks and come up with a statement to help you stay focused on them.

2) Keep that list and statement in a visible place so that when you're tempted not to do the disliked task you allow what you get from doing the task to propel you forward.

3) If you can't do it alone, get help. I just got help and it feels great. Let me explain: I have been thinking about and working on writing this book for two years, but have never "felt" like writing (kind of a problem). Finally, I got tired of my excuses. I got tired of draining my energy by thinking about it. I got tired of rationalizing that because I am a coach I should be able to keep myself accountable and write my book alone. I got tired of this goal hanging over my head, cluttering my mental space and decided to do something about it. So I signed up for a course called Write Your Book in a Weekend™. Daunting? Yes. Exciting? Yes! Now I would have accountability and could finally get my book done.

Since you are reading this you know my strategy worked. If you find you cannot complete your disliked tasks no matter how intent you are on doing them, like me, it's time for you to seek out and put some accountability structures in place. Make a list of possible structures such as professional help, a friend, a planner, rewards, etc. and choose one. After some consistent activity you will feel lighter, more confident, and better about yourself. Who knows, you may even start to "feel like" doing these tasks.

## Notes

# Conclusion

I want you to know I believe in you! If you have a vision for your business I know you can make it happen. Have patience with yourself, others, and the process. Choose one attitude shift to work on at a time and incorporate that into your business. When you do you'll be one step closer to creating the business of your dreams. Don't wait, start today!

Below is a summary of the nine attitude shifts discussed in this book:

1) Don't run from things you are afraid to do. Move towards them. Remember if you are not scared you are not playing a big enough game.
2) Success is not to be measured in numbers. Measure it in the actions you take and the character qualities you display. Failure is inevitable. Change your perception of what it means to make a mistake.
3) Your energy is not finite. Protect it.
4) You are not an imposter, even if it feels that way. Take comfort in the fact that many other people feel this way too.
5) Change your definition of what it means to be a salesperson. You are responsible to people, not for their emotional responses.
6) Don't assume you know what others are thinking about you. Especially if it's negative.
7) Don't expect clients and prospects to follow up with you. Even if they are interested in what you offer. It's your job to follow up with them.

8) Never wait for motivation to set in. Take action instead.

9) When running a business you will have to do things you don't feel like doing. Do them.

# Author's Note: My Secret Sauce

This book on changing your mindset would not be complete if I did not share my "secret sauce." I decided to write this in my Author's Note instead of making it a chapter because this book is for everybody regardless of your faith. For me, the principles in the chapters have changed the way I look at life and how I behave. Yet I am very clear that it is my relationship with Jesus that has made permanent changes in my heart and mind.

Without prayer and the loving guidance of God, applying the principles in this book and truly incorporating them into my life would be exponentially more difficult. If you believe the same as me, I encourage you to lean on God to change your mindset and grow your business. If you believe differently maybe you want to check Him out. If you're not sure how to, feel free to contact me at coach@fireyourfear.com. I'd love to discuss this with you. Be assured I will respect wherever you are at in your journey. It is not my intent to tell you what to do but rather to share the love, hope, and support I've received since I committed my life to Christ eleven years ago.

# What's Next?

If you'd like information on booking Deirdre for your company or organization's next national or local event, please visit www.minneapolisbusinessspeaker.com or www.fireyourfear.com and click the speaking tab.

**Special Offer**

Visit www.fireyourfear.com to receive a bonus chapter on setting goals that are compatible with the way you think.

To sign up for Deirdre's monthly business-building Action Step visit www.fireyourfear.com.

# Acknowledgements

Profound gratitude to my family, both immediate and extended who have always believed in me and encouraged me to follow my dreams.

To my friends, who make me laugh and pick me up when I am down.

To Elizabeth DeKlavon, an amazing young woman with a bright future. Not only did she edit this book, she helped shape it and brought it to life.

To Donna Kozik whose Write a Book in a Weekend™ seminar helped me get this done.

To all the professionals involved in helping me write this book. I couldn't have done it without your expertise and support.

To my amazing clients. It is a privilege to serve you.

Most of all to God, my loving Father. You never leave me nor forsake me. You are my hope.

# About the Author

Deirdre Van Nest is a Certified Fearless Living Coach, and a Get Clients Now!™ facilitator. She is an expert at helping others Fire their Fear! Often times we have put fear in charge of making decisions for us. Deirdre shows you how to recognize where fear is showing up in your life and gives you the tools to fire it from the role of executive decision maker. Her experience as a coach confirms that fear, lack of focus, and lack of support are the number one reasons people stay stuck and often feel like they are surviving rather than thriving.

In 1998, Deirdre earned her Master's degree in Occupational Therapy. Then in 2001, she started a real estate investment company. Since 2007 she has worked as a speaker and a coach, helping hundreds of professionals grow their businesses by changing the way they think. Deirdre knows firsthand that you must develop a certain mindset and certain disciplines in order to consistently and effectively promote yourself, your business, and your skills.

Made in the USA
Charleston, SC
09 May 2012